Build Your Dollhouse Apartment Building

Plan Book: Doll House Apartment Building; Unlimited Floors

By Dollhouse Devotions

All rights reserved.

No part of this publication may be reproduced in any form or by any means, including scanning, photocopying, or otherwise without prior written permission of the copyright holder.

Disclaimer and Terms of Use: The Author and Publisher has strived to be as accurate and complete as possible in the creation of this book, notwithstanding the fact that he does not warrant or represent at any time that the contents within are accurate due to the rapidly changing nature of the Internet. While all attempts have been made to verify information provided in this publication, the Author and Publisher assumes no responsibility for errors, omissions, or contrary interpretation of the subject matter herein.

As with any craft book, care needs to be taken when working with anything sharp, chemical based or anything else craft related. The Author and Publisher are not responsible for any injury relating to the use of craft supplies.

You are given a non-transferable, "personal use" license to this product. You cannot distribute it or share it with other individuals.

Also, there are no resale rights or private label rights granted when purchasing this document. In other words, it's for your own personal use only.

The original illustrations and plans for this book came from works by Robert Nealy. Additional illustrations and updated instructions have been provided by Dollhouse Devotions.

Build Your Own Dollhouse Apartment Building

Plan Book: Doll House Apartment Building; Unlimited Floors

By Dollhouse Devotions

Table of Contents

Introduction 7
General Instructions 10
    Patterns 10
    Foam Core 11
    Wood 11
    Nails 12
    Illustration Board 13
    Turnings 14
    Trim 16

Three Story Apartment Building 17
    Important Info 18
    Base 20
    Floor Plans 22
    Center 24
    Bay Window 27
    Sides 33
    Side 1 35
    Side 2 38
    The Lip 40
    Roof 42
    Chimney 47

Finishing Touches 49
    Floors 49
    Wall Pictures 51
    Brick 52
    Shingles 53
    Doors 53
    Stained Glass 54
    Wallpaper 54

Introduction

From simple one-room cottages, to log cabins, to Colleen Moore's Fairy Tale Castle, there's just something about a dollhouse that appeals to the child in us all.

In days gone by, the dollhouse was a true work of art, something you would be proud to display to friends and family. They were the realms of adults, not children.

These days, there are more 'kit' houses available than ever before. However, the modern miniaturist isn't looking for a kit house. The dollhouse collector and artist wants something more challenging, more inspirational.

They want something more like the dollhouses of days gone by. They want a dollhouse that's a work of art.

This book series will introduce you to some of the most popular and the most unusual dollhouses of days gone by.

These books have been specially designed to look like a plan book from yesteryear. From their creamy papers to their charming hand drawn illustrations, to their faux woven cover, everything is designed to give you an experience like few other books can.

Important info will be at the beginning of each project. It will give you a list of materials, the difficulty level, the size of the house according to the measurements and how easy it can be replicated in foam core.

At the end of each book there are some easy decorating ideas such as hardwood floors and carpets and shingles.

Every lover of dollhouses wants a dollhouse as beautiful and unique as the treasures it contains and this book will provide hours of fun as you create the perfect dollhouse for all your treasures.

****

As a crafter and dollhouse lover myself, I know what a hassle it is to try to copy patterns out of books.

That's why I've included a link that enables you to download all the patterns in this book in reduced size PDF form.

You can use your computer or copier to adjust them to whatever size you need.

Simply scan the QR code below or go to this website to get your PDF patterns:

http://www.thisofferisgreat.com/dollhouseaptbuilding

General Instructions

Patterns

This book contains patterns and illustrations for all the dollhouses.

The patterns in this series come in a variety sizes. While many are for 1:12 houses, others are not.

Fortunately, you can actually make these houses any size you want by making minor adjustments and enlarging the pattern to the size you need.

While measurements don't need to be quite as exact as the ones given here, precise measurements do give a wonderful 'starting point' for your ultimate creation.

Foam Core

Though traditional dollhouses are made of wood, I have always preferred foam core due to its ease of use. The instructions for each house are for wood. However, they can also be made out of foam core with relative ease. For each house, I mention the level of difficulty involved with following the instructions to turn it into a foam core house rather than a wooden one.

Wood

It all starts with the wood. What kind of wood you choose is ultimately decided by what kind of dollhouse you want. A dollhouse that will be completely covered in wallpaper and brick can use very rough wood, such as plywood. However, a dollhouse that's going to be finely finished and painted should use a wood of higher quality.

The highest quality wood for dollhouses is basswood. Even though it's among the most expensive, the finished result is truly an heirloom quality house.

If price is a concern, you can choose less-expensive wood, like pine. Pine can still give you a finely finished heirloom quality dollhouse for a fraction of the cost of basswood. Additionally, being a soft wood, it's still very easy to work with.

The most important thing to remember when working with pine or other woods is to make sure it's free from knots and other out of scale defects that could ruin the overall look of your perfect house.

Nails

Because this is not a real house, we can use smaller nails that leave easy to fill holes.

While screws will give you the sturdiest house, finishing nails will give you an overall smooth appearance and can be punched in with an awl.

Once punched in, finishing nails are easily covered up with a little bit of wood putty, sandpaper and paint.

Illustration Board

Illustration board is available at many fine art stores and is wonderful for a variety of purposes. Illustration board is actually a type of compressed cardboard. It is sturdy and easy to cut with a craft knife.

Illustration board is easy to curve around things. To curve illustration board, use a craft knife to lightly score the illustration board as shown by the dotted lines below.

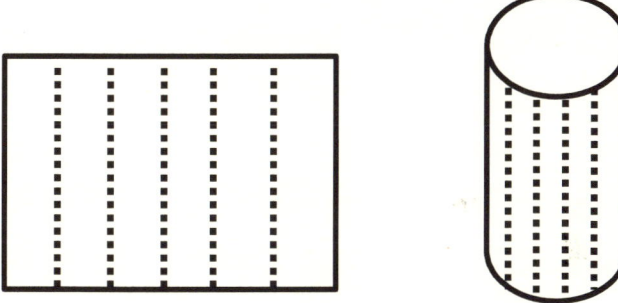

Once you've scored the illustration board, curve the illustration board away from the lines instead of toward.

This method can be used for creating columns, arches, tubes and bowed windows.

Cardstock can then be wrapped around the piece and finished as desired.

Turnings

Throughout this book, you'll notice references to 'turnings'. Turnings are fancy, 3 dimensional, freestanding, carved woodwork.

Example of turnings

Turnings can be used in a variety of places in your dollhouse, including:

- Stair railings
- Poster Beds
- Architectural columns
- Furniture legs
- More...

In this book, we use them primarily for creating railings for stairs.

Real wood turnings can be bought relatively cheaply at just about any dollhouse supply store or catalogue.

You can find a section of online resources in the back of the books where you can buy turnings.

However, for the truly creative, you can use beads to simulate wood turnings.

These beads can be either wood or plastic. Carved beads, such as ethnic beads make a particularly good looking carved 'turning'.

Simply stack beads on top of each other until you get the size and shape that you want. Glue them in place. Then paint the beads to resemble wood.

Turning made from beads

Just like with wood turnings, these bead 'turnings' can give you a wonderful effect and can be used for furniture feet, elaborate carvings, columns and posters on a four poster bed.

Trim

Trim can go either on the inside or outside of the dollhouse. It can be the molding next to the floorboards, the ceiling or the outside of the house.

It can also go around the windows, doors and porches.

Though you can buy regular wood trim from your favorite dollhouse retailer, there are other ways to simulate trim.

Heavily textured lace or embossed papers work well as trim. In addition, lace has the added benefit of being able to bend around curves and corners without needing to be mitered.

Deeply Etched Lace

Heavily textured lace, like the lace in the picture, works best for this.

Three Story Apartment Building

stylish & modern apartment building

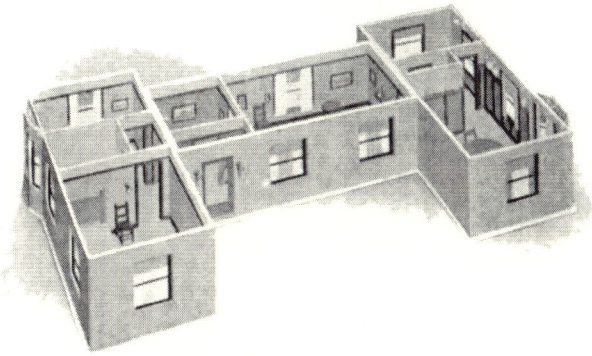

a single 6-room apartment, one floor

Important Info:

Size of house:
- Varies according to preference

Level of difficulty:
- Easy to intermediate

Can be reproduced in foam core:
- Easily

Materials:
- Sheets of wood (and tools for wood)
- Glue
- Strip wood
- Plastic sheet glass
- Illustration board (board)
- Cardstock (Card)
- T-square (or carpenters ruler)
- Pencil

Something you rarely see in the dollhouse world is a dollhouse apartment building.

This is a shame as an apartment building solves the age-old problem of having to stay with one style in your dollhouse.

Because each apartment has its own kitchen, living room, bedrooms and bathroom, the decorating opportunity is unlimited.

These plans show you how to make one floor of the apartment and a roof. Though the picture is one of a 3-story building, each apartment floor is freestanding and comes with its own façade. This means that you can keep adding as many floors as you want for as long as you want.

In fact, your dollhouse apartment building could even become a long-term project.

Since the roof and apartments aren't attached, you can continually add new floors every time you feel like decorating in a different style.

The best thing about this dollhouse is that since it grows 'up' instead of 'out', you never have to worry about it occupying more space than it currently does.

Base

You'll notice this house is shaped like an extended 'H'. This unique configuration allows for a small vestibule, a reception hall, and a living room in the main part of the house.

While the center part of the 'H' is considered the main part, it is also the narrowest part of the house. That makes it easy to decorate.

Trace the pattern shown in Figure 245 onto your wood. Once you've cut out the pattern, trace and mark where all the rooms go.

The pattern is almost identical on every floor except for on the first floor.

On the first floor there will be a door instead of a bay window. However, the same pattern is used.

The rest of the rooms, such as the bedrooms, kitchen and dining room, are laid out in the same way on all floors.

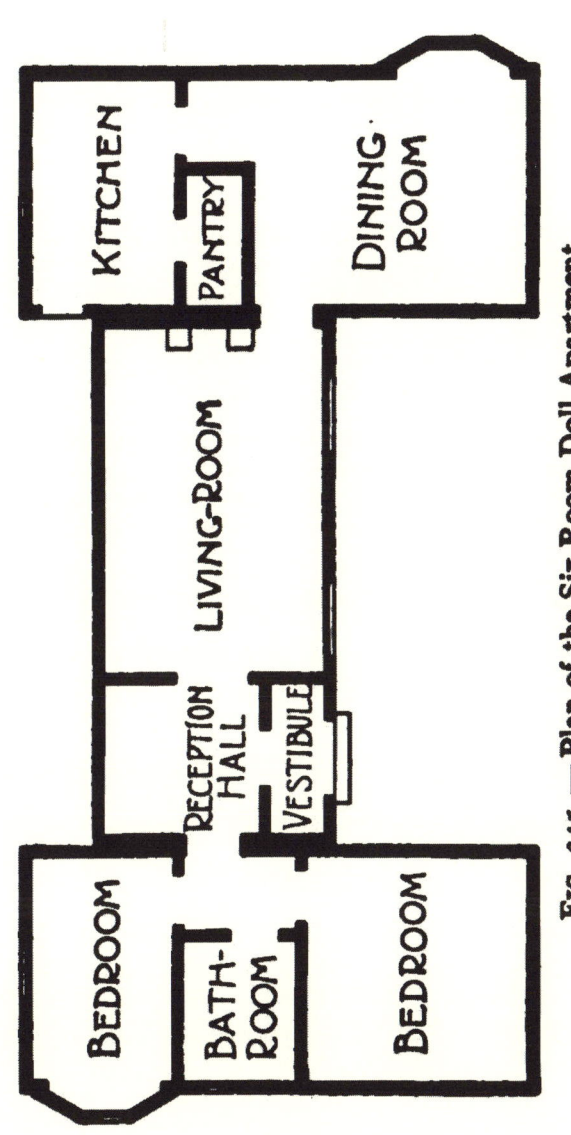

FIG. 245.—Plan of the Six-Room Doll Apartment.

Floor Plans

The floor plans of the rooms are as follows in the following illustration.

Each of these 3 sections are built separately then attached at the end.

Center

The center part shown in figure 246 shows the layout and partitions for this crossbar of the H. Notice that partitions A and B are placed to the far right. This enables you to have a small vestibule and reception area while still maintaining a large living room. Simply layout the patterns and mark and assemble as shown.

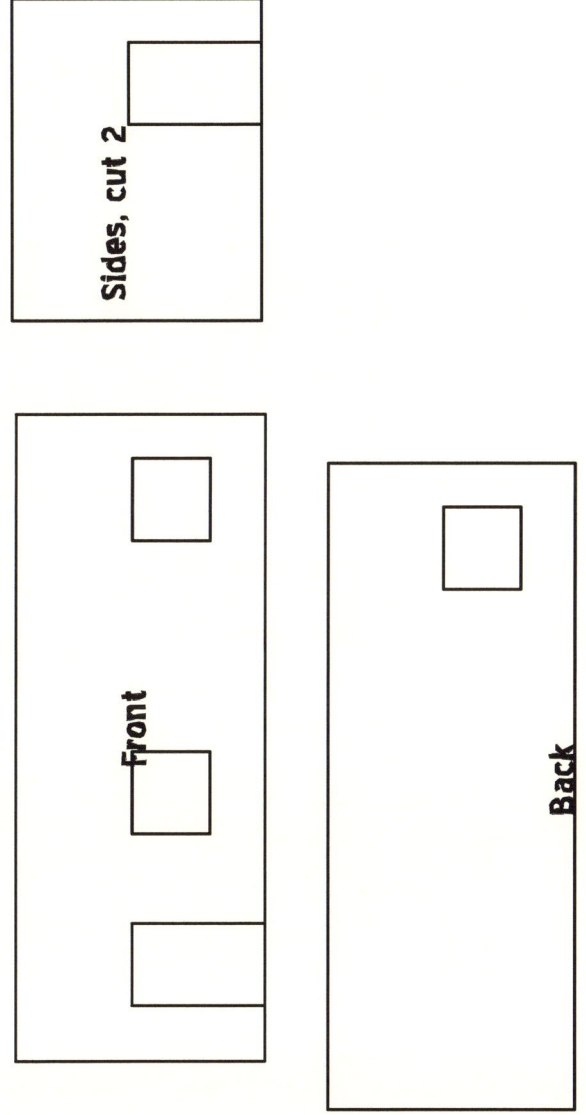

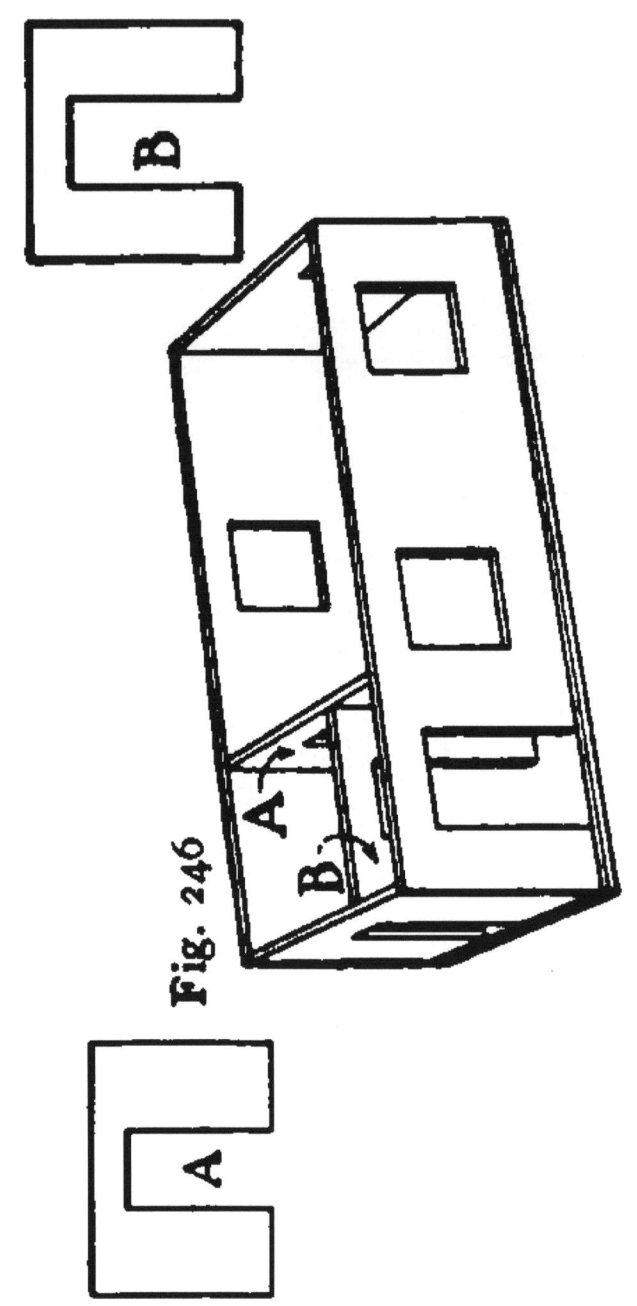

Fig. 246

Bay Window

Both side 1 and side 2 have a bay window. Therefore, the bay window is a great place to start.

When making a bay window, don't extend it all the way to the floor. It's actually much stronger if you leave a narrow strip of wood along both the top and the bottom.

These extra beams do not detract from the charm of the apartment, and give it added strength and stability it needs to support this window.

You can see this clearly in figure 249.

FIG. 249.—In Cutting the Opening for the Bay Windows, leave a Narrow Strip over the Opening, as above, for a "Beam."

To make the bay window itself, you can use thin strip wood or board.

Thick wood needs to be mitered in order to properly fit. Using thin wood or board eliminates the need for mitering.

To make a bay window, cut out 1 of pattern A and 2 of pattern B. This makes one bay window.

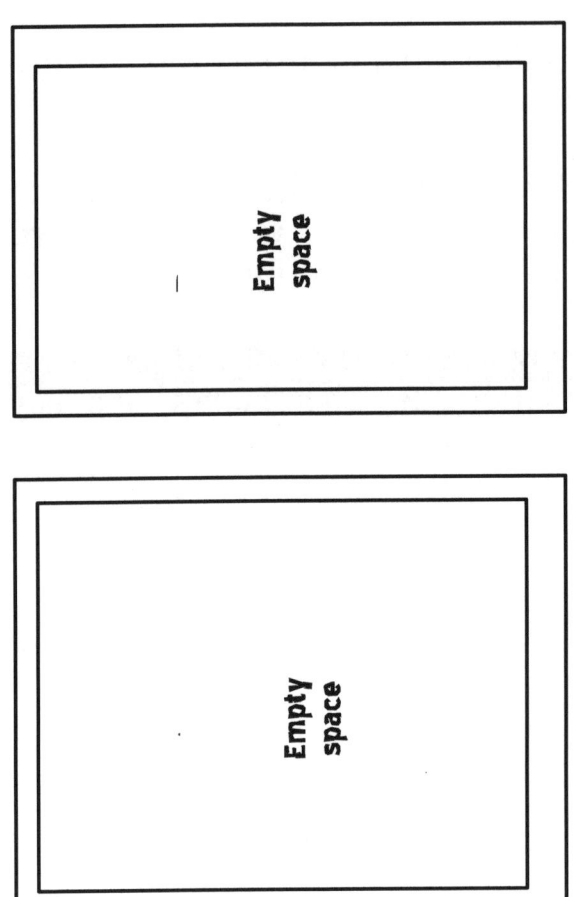

When cutting out the patterns for the window, leave the center of the wood cutouts empty. This is where the window glass will go.

Window 'glass' for dollhouses can be easily purchased. It's sold as sheets of thin plastic.

This plastic sheet (sometimes known as 'plastic sheet glass') is easily cut with a craft knife or scissors.

Cut the plastic sheet glass just a little bit bigger than the window opening so it overlaps slightly onto the frame.

Glue this glass directly to the frame.

Window casements are built directly on the house. These casements go on both the inside and the outside to give the illusion of an entire window.

These casements are built with thin strip wood or board.

Assemble as shown in the picture. Narrow strips of wood or craft matchsticks placed directly on the plastic sheet glass will give the impression of divided glass.

A roof for the window is not necessary because the top of the bay window will be made up by the bottom of the next floor. This continues until you reach the roof.

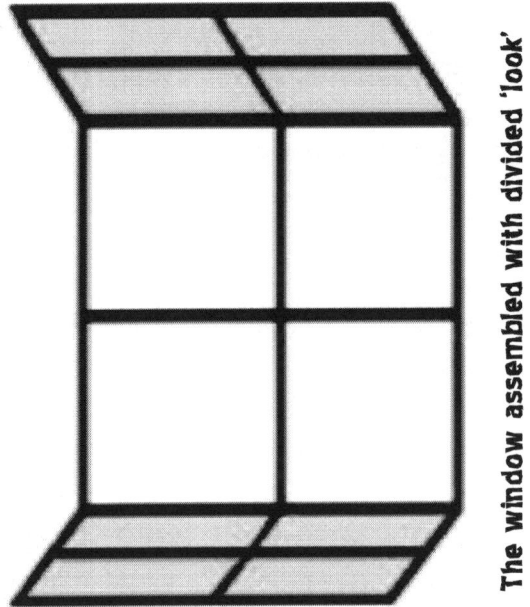

The window assembled with divided 'look'

Sides

Side 1 and side 2 actually use the same basic patterns for the exterior. Though they vary on the interior, they are mirror images of each other, with the bay window being on the front on one side and the back of the other.

The doors shown on the exterior part of the pattern are where the bay windows go

To make the other sides, cut 2 each of the pattern and 4 of the small pattern below and remember that one side will be reversed.

This matters if you're using wood that has a 'good side'.

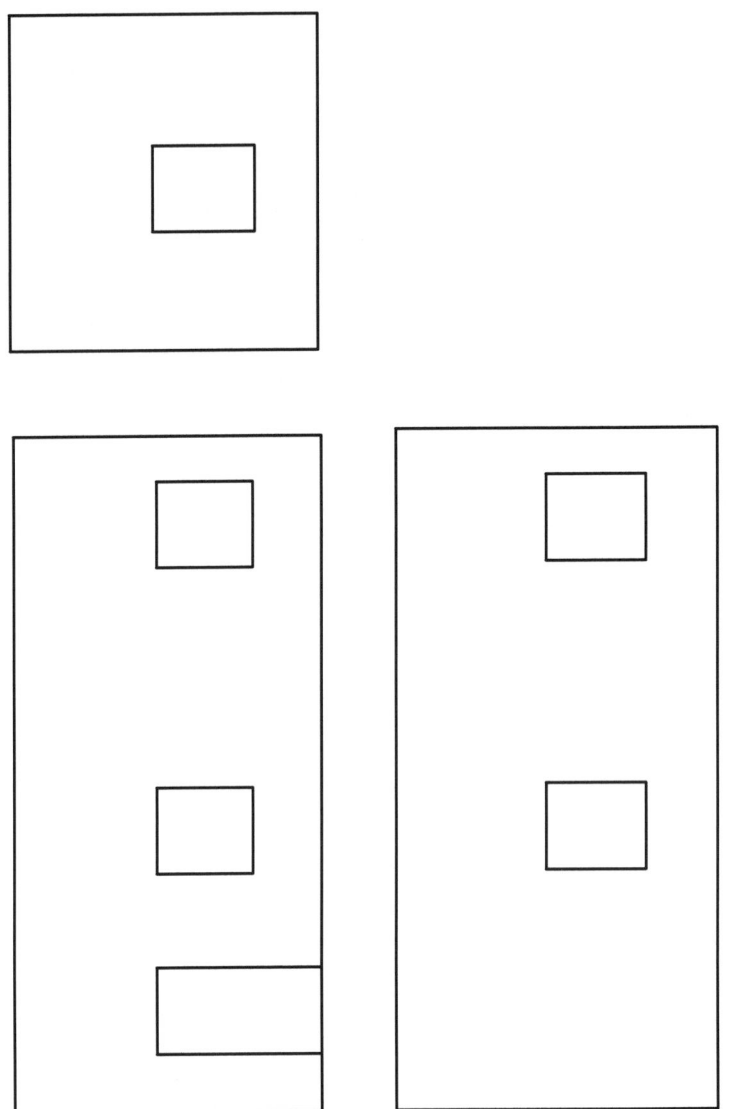

Side 1

Once you have cut out all the patterns, build the side as seen in figure 247.

This side has three partitions; C, D and E

These partitions are placed to the far right and left. Cut out the partitions and arrange them as shown in Figure 247.

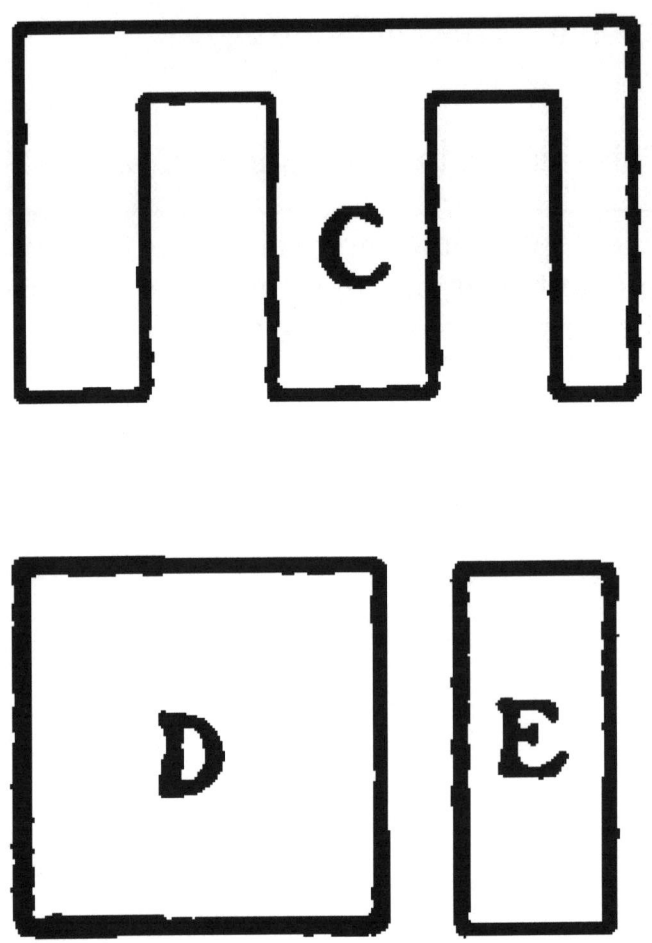

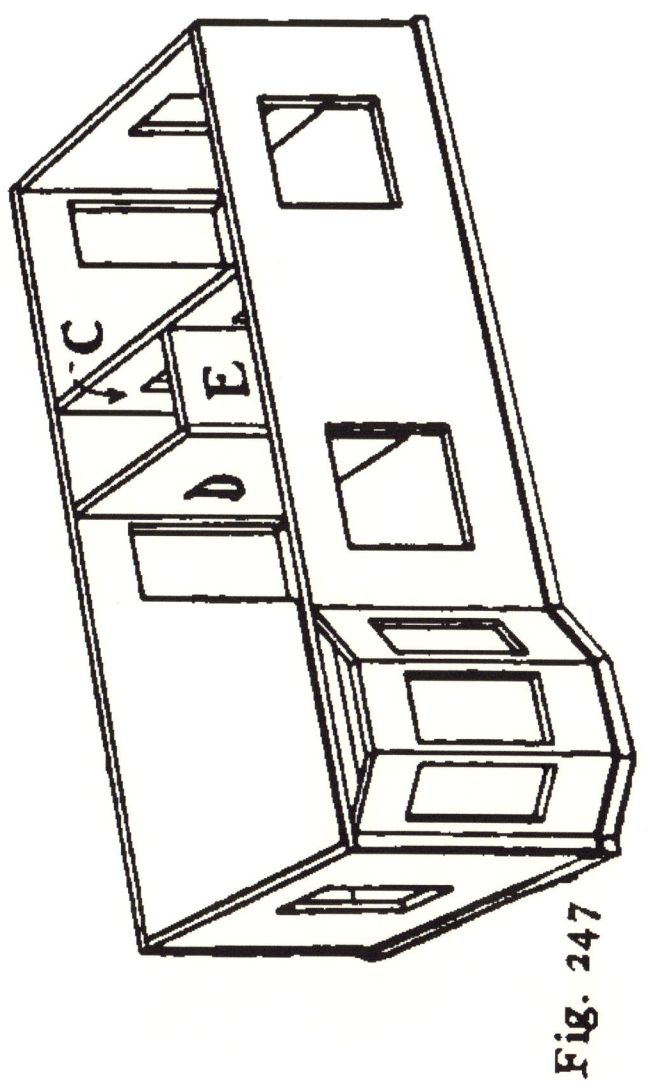

Fig. 247

Side 2

Side 2 only has two partitions, F and G. Now that you've built side one, repeat the process for side 2, keeping in mind that this side will be reversed. Cut and place the partitions as shown in Figure 248.

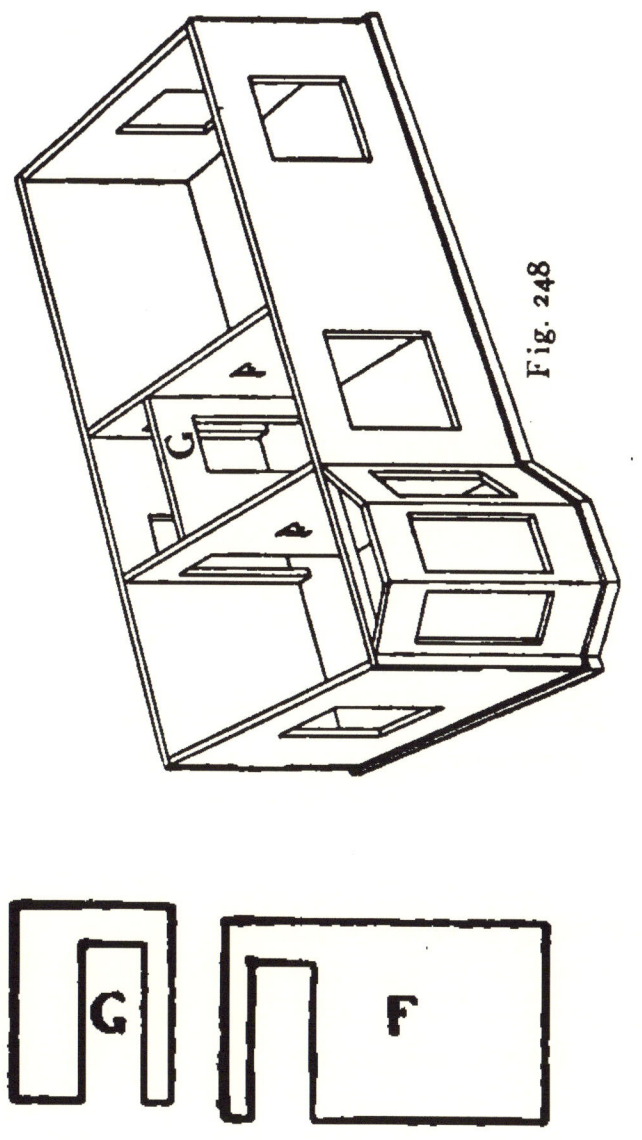

The Lip

To keep the stories in place, it becomes necessary to add special 'joints'. This way, the apartment building won't topple over as it grows.

The joints used here are the simplest kind of joint, known as a 'lip'.

This simple 'joint' works by slightly overlapping the floor beneath it. This keeps the floors on top in place.

To create a lip, use a sturdy strip of wood between ¼- ½" wide. This is one of the rare occasions where board will not work.

Run this band of wood all the way around the apartment floors as shown in figure 260. Cut and add more strips as necessary.

You can finish the lips as you would the rest of the building so it will blend.

You can also draw attention to the lip by turning it into an architectural detail. Many older apartment buildings have tiny 'friezes' between floors. To create a frieze effect, you can use beads, rhinestones or puffy paint.

Then paint the lip to resemble plaster or stone.

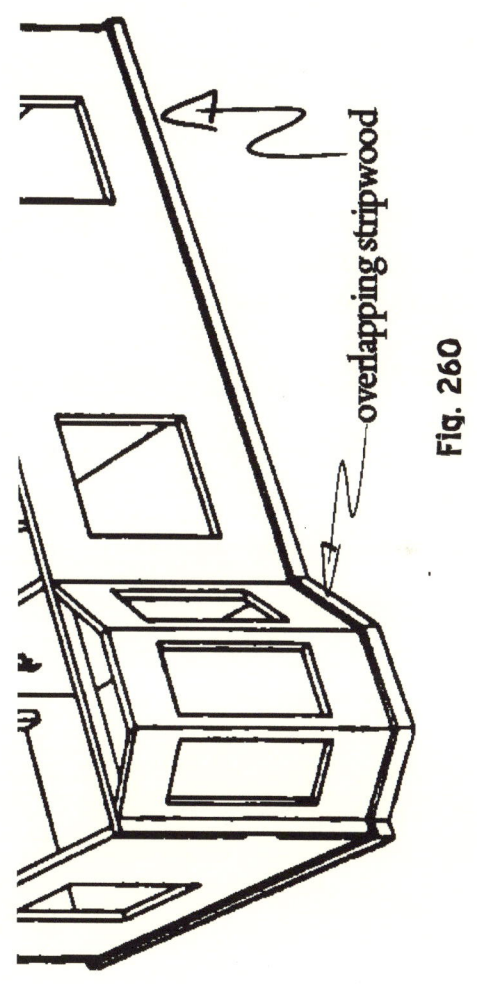

Fig. 260

Roof

Figure 250 shows the construction of the roof. This roof is actually built upside down. Once the roof is done, it will be flipped as shown to fit snugly within the apartment building.

For the sake of simplicity and clarity, the roof pictured is one part of the total roof.

This roof can either be made as three separate pieces to be attached later, as figure 251 shows, or as one solid piece.

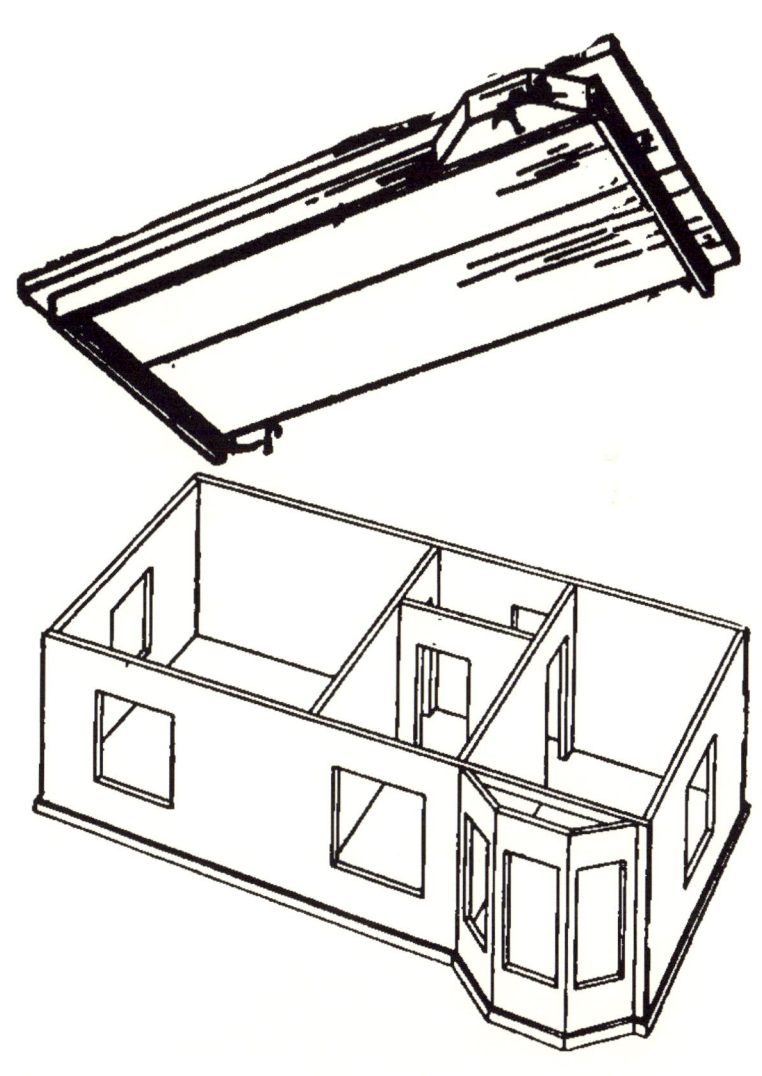

Fig. 251
1 part of a 3 part roof

To make the roof as one single piece, reuse the same pattern you used to create the base.

If you are planning to create the roof in parts, create a pattern by tracing the tops of each section of the apartment.

The roof should stick out about 1 ½" over the front and sides of the building.

If you cut a rectangular roof, there is still a way to overlap the bay window.

Piece I is an extra piece that can be cut separately and then attached. This forms the projection over the bay window. This projection should overlap the bay window by the same amount as the rest of the roof.

Piece I

Strips J and K are an inch wide and should be placed slightly in front of the actual walls of the apartment building.

Strips J and K are creating an interior overhang to ensure a snug fit of the roof.

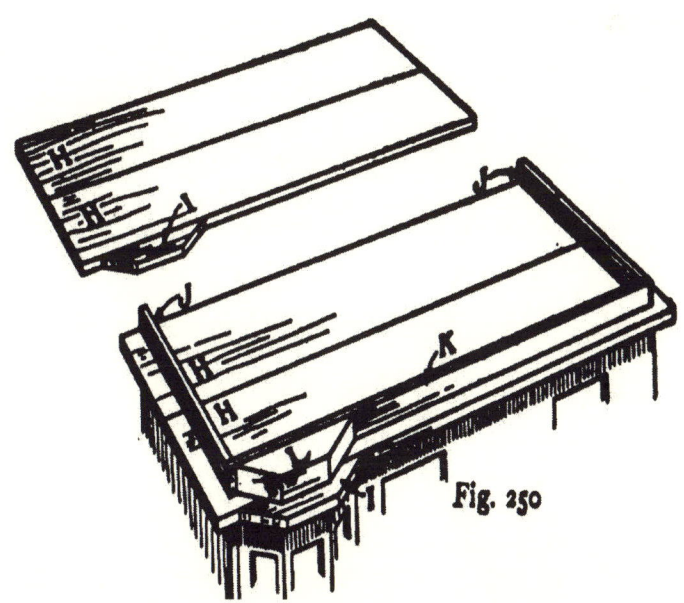
Fig. 250

Once the roof is built, flip it as shown in the picture before making the chimney.

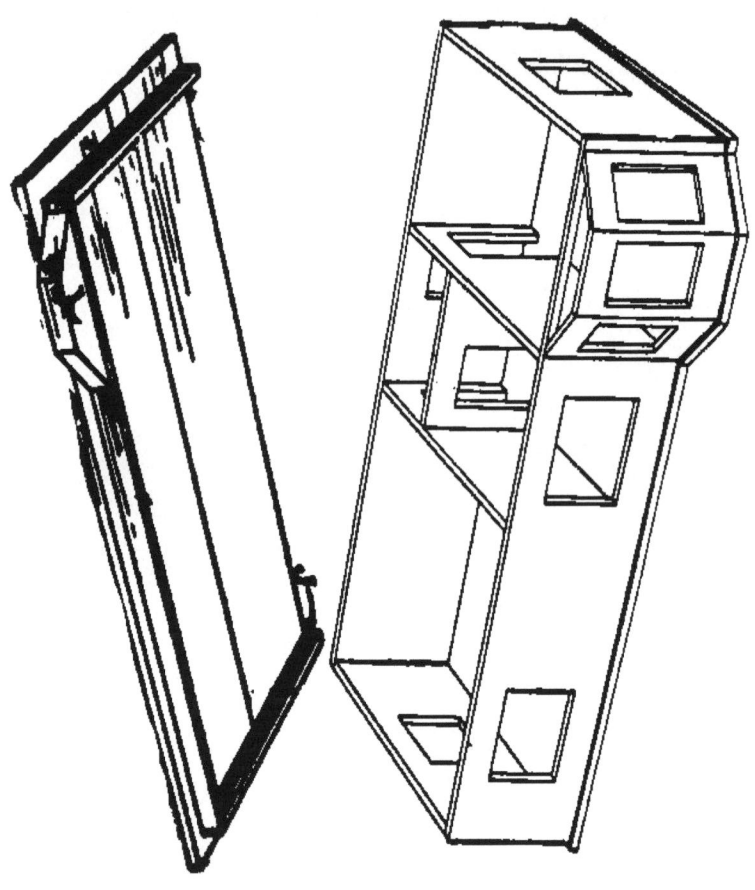

Chimney

Chimneys are optional on apartment buildings.

However, they do add a bit more architectural interest than a simple flat roof.

The chimney for this apartment building is much simpler than the chimney for a dollhouse with a slanted roof.

The chimney is actually two blocks, as seen in figure 252. These two blocks are M and N. M is the main part of the chimney, while N is the chimney cap.

To create M, simply choose a small block of wood that is the size you want.

Most apartment buildings have thin modern chimneys instead of old-fashioned wide ones.

Fig. 252

Once you've chosen your chimney block, attach a flat piece of wood that overlaps the chimney on all sides.

This creates your chimney cap.

Interior doors are optional.

You will find more on doors and making brick under the *'Finishing Touches'* section of this book.

Congratulations!

You've Just Finished the First Floor and Roof of Your Dollhouse Apartment!

Finishing Touches

Now we come to one of the most fun parts about having a dollhouse; the decorating. While this is by no means a comprehensive chapter on decorating, decorating alone could fill a book; this will give you a brief overview on how to finish your dollhouse so you can have one you're proud of.

Floors

There are several options for floors in your dollhouse. Which one you choose will depend on your personal taste.

Using Your Home's Natural Wood

If your dollhouse is made of real wood, then you can you can simply use a craft knife and ruler to score the floor so it looks like planks. When you stain the floor, the stain will naturally collect in these grooves giving the illusion of actual planks.

Popsicle Sticks

To make an inexpensive real wood floor, use popsicle sticks with the round ends cut off. Glue them down, and then stain as usual.

Commercial Hardwood Floors

Hardwood floors are available commercially. They are made up thin woods applied to a fabric backing. Since they are genuine, often exotic, woods, they are the most expensive option.

Floorpaper

For a more economical alternative to real wood or tile, consider floorpaper. Floorpaper simulates the look of tile, wood, parquet and more.

Best of all, you can buy whole books of floorpaper for the price of the most commercially available hardwood floors.

To see the selection of floorpaper available from Dollhouse Devotions, go to:

http://www.thisofferisgreat.com/dd

Carpets and Rugs

Carpets can either be bought commercially or simulated with felt.

Throw rugs can be purchased, created with fancy ribbons, scraps of appropriately textured cloth or old fashioned handkerchiefs.

Tile

Tile has to be small enough in scale both thinness and surface. Polymer clay is an excellent choice for tile because it can be created paper thin.

Plastic dollhouse tile sheets or tiled floorpaper are also good options.

Wall Pictures

No home is complete without pictures.

Pictures can be cut out of magazines and then framed with strip wood to give the illusion of a picture in a frame.

These frames can even be embellished with puffy paint or small rhinestones painted a solid color to represent a fancier frame.

You can also use paper frames to show off your mini artwork.

Brick

There are commercial brick kits you can buy to give the illusions of bricks. These kits feature everything from individual clay bricks to stencils and textured paint.

You can also use sand paper cut into brick shapes and painted the appropriate color. These paper bricks have the advantage of being able to turn around corners.

Brick paper can also be used if you want to cover a large area quickly. Like floorpaper, brick paper is the most economical alternative. Either you can buy sheets of brick paper or you can purchase a book of floorpaper that has the appropriate brick pattern in it.

Shingles

In addition to commercially available shingles, there are many other ways to shingle a house.

Again, sand paper can be used by cutting into the appropriate strips and gluing it into place.

Shingle paper can also be used if you're looking to cover large areas quickly.

Doors

Though doors can be purchased commercially, they can also be made with thin stripwood or board.

These handcrafted doors can be created with pieces of board, strip wood, rhinestones or even puffy paint. Simply apply your embellishments and paint to look like wood or painted wood.

A fabric hinge is easily made by gluing a piece of fabric to both the door and the interior of the door way. This hinge can then be covered with trim, wallpaper or paint.

A shiny bead can serve as doorknob.

Stained Glass

This can easily be replicated by printing out the appropriate patterns on computer transparency paper. When you download the patterns for this dollhouse, you will receive some stained glass patterns in a few days. Size to fit, then print out.

Wallpaper

Wallpaper is one of the most popular ways to finish the inside of a dollhouse. While sheets of wallpaper are available individually, wallpaper books can be purchased at a fraction of the price.

Be sure to check out Dollhouse Devotions' assortment of wallpaper books here:

http://www.thisofferisgreat.com/dd

A Note from Dollhouse Devotions:

If you enjoyed this book, please consider leaving a review.

If you have any suggestions on how to make future books better, you can contact us at:

info@newartspublishing.com

You can also download your free patterns from this book at

http://www.thisofferisgreat.com/dollhouseaptbuilding

Don't forget to see all our dollhouse books including floor plans and wallpapers.

http://www.thisofferisgreat.com/dd

Printed in Great Britain
by Amazon.co.uk, Ltd.,
Marston Gate.